pock
issue

Designed for our time-pressed lives, Pocket Issue's short and pithy handbooks pull together the background to some of the biggest challenges facing our world — delivering the facts in an independent and quick-to-digest format.

Praise for Pocket Issue:

'A brilliant wheeze: the essence of the debate in a very approachable format.' Harriet Lane, The Observer

'Exactly what any busy person needs - the facts at your fingertips! Never get caught out again when a conversation starts on the big issues of our time.' Jeremy Vine, BBC Radio 2 and Panorama

'For everyone who longs to be well-informed but lacks the time (or attention span).' Alex Clark, The Observer

'Prep yourself by keeping the one on global warming in the downstairs loo...' Mary Killen, The Spectator

'Precisely what's needed...' Hephzibah Anderson, The Daily Mail

Dig deeper on any issue we cover through our blog, plus find out about new publications and special offers on our website, www.pocketissue.com. And tell us what you think, we always welcome your suggestions and comments.

Now available in Audio — order online at www.talkingissues.com.

Pocket issue
Small briefs for a big world

Big Brother
who is watching you?

Published by Pocket Issue, London
www.pocketissue.com
info@pocketissue.com

Copyright © Pocket Issue, 2008
First edition, published November 2008.

ISBN: 0-9554415-9-5
ISBN: 978-0-9554415-9-2

The contents of this publication are believed to be correct at
the time of printing. Nevertheless, the publisher can accept no
responsibility for errors or omissions, changes in the details given,
or for any expense or loss thereby caused.

Design by Studio 176.
info@studio176.co.uk

Production by Francois Weideman.
www.writedesign.co.za

Each Pocket Issue follows a similar format and for *Big Brother: who is watching you?* we would like to thank the following team:

Author: Joseph O'Neill
Illustration: Andrzej Krauze
Production design: Francois Weideman
Editorial: Mary Alexander, Emma Hardcastle, Victoria Dean

We would also like to thank those who have offered help and advice along the way:
Dolores O'Neill, Joanna Everard, Julia Bullock, Nick Band, Flo Bayley, Dr Jonathan Parry, Richard Sunderland.

About the author

Author Joseph O'Neill is a freelance author and broadcaster whose work has featured in all the major family history magazines. He writes a regular feature for the BBC's *Who Do You Think You Are?* and is author of *Crime City*, his account of Manchester's Victorian underworld.

The Pocket Issue Team

Contents

One minute guide

The big issues in the blink of an eye

One minute guide

Well known as the TV show based on the concept of 24 hour surveillance of a group of people locked up in a house together, but the phrase 'Big Brother' also has more sinister and serious connotations than entertainment for the masses. Do you know who's watching you and why? Just one minute to spare? Read on for some key facts.

What is Big Brother?

Big Brother symbolises an all-powerful state, monitoring our actions and thoughts and immediately crushing any opposition with its absolute power. This power is so intrusive that any form of private life is impossible.

Where does the phrase 'Big Brother' come from?

George Orwell coined it in his 1949 novel Nineteen Eighty-Four. It immediately became widely used.

Why was Orwell so concerned about the all-powerful state?

Britain and her allies had recently defeated Hitler's tyrannical dictatorship in Germany. Yet even after Germany's defeat there still existed in the USSR and throughout the Soviet-dominated governments behind the Iron Curtain equally sinister regimes. By the 1950s the East German secret police, the Stasi, employed one informer for every six citizens. Orwell wanted people to realise the dangers of the state using blanket surveillance to destroy individual freedom in order to maintain absolute control over the population.

Why do we hear so much about the Big Brother state today?

Many people are concerned because the surveillance technology Big Brother used in Nineteen Eighty-Four, which was the stuff of science fiction in 1949, is now reality. American writer David Ross claims that fifty years after Orwell's death, of the 137 'total surveillance' predictions made in Nineteen-Eighty-Four, 100 have come true. Civil liberties campaigners see the national ID card as a major step towards a surveillance society.

Are governments using this technology? Many governments, but particularly the British government, are using this technology to keep the population under constant surveillance. Governments have the capacity to collate and analyse the resulting data in a way even Orwell didn't foresee.

Who else is spying on us? Commercial organisations use information to target us with their goods and services. Thousands of businesses own or acquire detailed information on millions of people, which they 'mine' for trends. Criminals also use our personal information, now held in so many places, to commit identity fraud and steal our money and reputation.

How is this happening? There are 4.5 million Closed Circuit Television (CCTV) cameras in Britain, one for every 14 of us. Menwith Hill in Yorkshire, the largest electronic monitoring station in the world, tracks every telephone conversation in Europe, North Africa and Western Asia.

Driving somewhere? Think your Sat Nav is good news? Orbital satellites that can pick out any one of us and watch where we go use the same technology. Vehicles in London are monitored by the London congestion charging technology while many motorways have cameras every 400 yards.

Going to the shops? Every time you use your credit or debit card your purchase is logged and the retailer can discover your address, bank details and credit worthiness, amongst other things.

You cannot be serious…? Oh yes. Privacy is thin on the ground in the 21st century. Even visiting your doctor isn't private these days: every trip is registered on the NHS database which charts our health history over the course of our lives and is available to the Secretary of State for Health and whoever he decides should view it. The National DNA database has 4 million citizens registered on it, including 500,000 children under 16.

Eavesdropping Any one of us can buy a digital voice recorder for less than £100, which pinpoints and records conversations in crowded public areas. Such devices are routinely used to impinge on people's privacy. "I don't know any famous person who hasn't had their conversations tapped," said Liz Hurley.

Anyone else who wants to know what I'm up to? Everything you do on the Internet involves using a server, which retains a record of your activities from requesting a page to opening an email. As a result Government Information Services and commercial businesses now hold a vast amount of information on us all.

Why does the government want this information? To combat terrorist threats, protect national security, prevent unwanted immigration, tackle crime, and to provide services to the population such as education and health care.

That's all very well but what about our civil liberties? Laws like the Data Protection Act and the Freedom of Information Act protect us in theory, but civil liberties groups claim that in practice these have been dramatically eroded, and will continue to be as further monitoring measures are introduced.

Espresso

So the coffee is being passed around and your host is looking serene. Here are some things you should (and shouldn't) say to keep your place at the table.

Have a second helping

"History proves that the price of freedom is eternal vigilance."

"It's impossible today for law-abiding people to go about their business without being spied on."

"I'm fed up with being bombarded with offers for fishing tackle just because I once Googled 'salmon in the Mersey.'

"The amount of personalised junk mail I get is doing significant harm to the rain forests."

Get your coat

"Big Brother is a thing of the past. Viewers are getting fed up with it and ratings are plummeting."

"Only those with something to hide worry about state surveillance."

"The state's first duty is to use every means at its disposal to protect its citizens. If that involves stepping on the toes of a few people, so be it."

"Technology is too powerful to control. Whether we like it or not, privacy is an outdated notion."

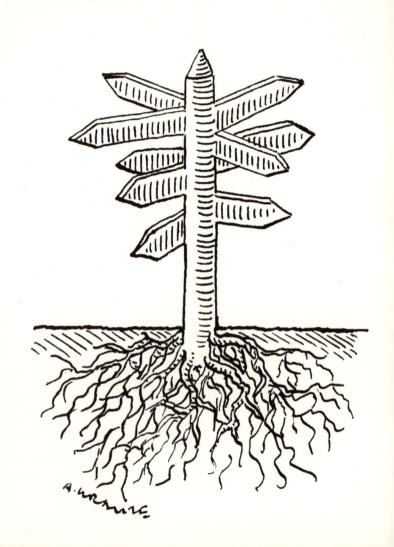

Roots

The important questions answered

Big Brother – what's the issue?

Big Brother is the all-seeing state, keeping everyone under surveillance, watching everything we do. Britain is the most watched society on earth - in terms of CCTV cameras per head - and London the most watched city. Cameras record and save images of virtually everything we do. The average person is filmed up to 300 times a day. The national ID card will eventually allow the government to monitor our movements in a way not possible since the Second World War. The Security Services can intercept and track any one of our phone calls.

To make matters worse, Big Brother has a commercial twin with an insatiable appetite for prying into our private lives. Every credit card purchase is logged and loyalty cards enable retailers to build up a detailed picture of you, which could then be sold on without your knowledge or permission to anybody prepared to pay for it. The average British adult is logged on about 700 databases.

Safe in your car? Think again. London congestion charging technology uses the sophisticated Automatic Number Plate Recognition system which matches plates with those linked to terrorists and criminals. Safe if you stay within the law? Technologies developed to counter crime are being rolled out to include the entire population. The National DNA database is growing at the rate of 60,000 people a month. Samples are now taken from anyone arrested for a recordable offence. Though most of the people on it have committed no crime their data will be kept for life.

Think your home is your castle? Not if you're logged on. Even when using your computer to trace your family tree or research an illness, you are being watched. Everything you do on the Internet involves using a server, which retains a record of your activities.

There is nowhere to hide.

The Rise of Big Brother

The term 'Big Brother', derived from George Orwell's book *Nineteen Eighty-Four*, appears almost daily in the media. It is shorthand for a type of government and society which deprives citizens of basic freedoms and individuality by controlling every aspect of life.

Britain's counter-espionage agency has existed at least since Elizabethan times when the state monitored those it regarded as a threat. In the last 60 years, Anglo-American co-operation for monitoring and interception has developed to such an extent that the two countries are now inextricably intertwined.

Technological developments have increased the government's capacity to spy on the population while the end of the Cold War together with increased fear of terrorism has led to this technology being used against the British population. ID Cards are becoming a reality. Pocket Issue gathers the facts.

When did the government start this systematic collecting of information? The Domesday Book was Britain's first census. William the Conqueror wanted to know the value of the kingdom he had won so in 1085 all heads of households and landowners were counted.

How did it develop from there? The next attempt to compile a record on the scale of the Domesday Book arrived only with the national census in 1801. In 1841 the government recorded information on named individuals and details of their occupation, religion and relationships.

How did the government counter threats to society? The police force dealt with crime and until the 19th century used only paper records and card indexes to record and cross-reference criminal information. For this reason many criminals were able to disguise their true identity by adopting an alias and thus avoid punishment as repeat offenders. This came to an end in 1869 with the Habitual Criminals Act, which introduced the photographing of criminals and established a central registry of identity. The first biometric data – fingerprints – used to identify criminals came into use at the end of the 19th century. As science developed, the police benefited – identifying blood groups and the presence of poisons in victims, using telegraph and telephone communication. But there was no systematic recording of information on people other than convicted criminals.

How did the government deal with the threat of enemy agents? In the First World War, the government introduced the National Registration Act, which required all those between 15 and 65 to enrol on a national register. The government assured opponents that people would not be required to produce a card and that the register would not be used to implement conscription, but later reneged on both promises.

Orwell was familiar with the National Registration Act (1939), which introduced ID cards. It was designed to identify enemy aliens – who were interned without trial – and to counter the threat of spies. He knew that during the Second World War the British government in fact become a dictatorship and suspended all democratic rights. It had the power to imprison without trial, control the media, confiscate property and spy on the population.

During the Second World War the British government become a dictatorship.

Who was responsible for spying on the population? By the start of the Second World War the British government already had in place the Secret Intelligence Service (MI6) and the Security Service (MI5). Then as now MI5 operated mainly in Britain, protecting the country from foreign spies and tracking subversives, terrorists, saboteurs, political activists and anyone else seen as a potential security threat.

What powers did the authorities have for spying on the population? Until 1937 the Post Office intercepted phone calls at the request of the police and the Special Branch – who worked with MI5 – since the Security Service had no power to actually make arrests without reference to a minister. After 1937 both phone tapping and mail opening could only be done when the Home Secretary issued a warrant. In theory the situation remains essentially unchanged, though now the Foreign Secretary and the Defence Secretary can also issue warrants.

How did things change during the Second World War? During the war the USA and Britain pooled all intelligence about the Germans and Japanese. Significantly, Churchill informed the Americans that Bletchley Park had broken the German Enigma cipher, used for all high-level communications.

The National Registration card was introduced at the beginning of the Second World War, in September 1939. It remained in use after the war, officially as an aid to administering the rationing system, until 1952.

How did the Cold War lead to increased surveillance? Britain and the USA became concerned by the success of communist spies and the consequent need to intercept the USSR's communications with subversive elements in the west. After 1945 the USA and her allies began assembling an enormous interception network. By the time Orwell wrote Nineteen Eighty-Four the Allies had already signed up to cooperate on signal interceptions by the USA's National Security Agency (NSA), Britain's

Government Communications Headquarter (GCHQ) and their Commonwealth counterparts. Each monitored a section of the globe. The major Cold War development to dwarf all others was RAF Menwith Hill.

The end of the Cold War and increased fears of terrorism have led to spying technology being used against the British population.

Why is this so important? It institutionalised the exchange of technical experts and the pooling of resources. Much of the technology presently used to monitor civilian populations was developed in the Cold War period, particularly in connection with satellite technology and the Star Wars developments. Menwith Hill got its first computer – one of the first produced by IBM – in 1965, which enabled it to make a major breakthrough into the automated interception of telex messages. From 1962 America put more and more intelligence-linked satellites into orbit until by 2000 Menwith Hill could intercept most of the world's mobile communications and signals intelligence.

How does it do this? Central to this is the Echelon system (see Glossary). It has the capacity to intercept 100,000 telephone calls at any one time. Additionally, a BT microwave transmitter, Hunter Stone Tower, which relays hundreds of thousands of calls, was built only four miles from Menwith Hill and is linked to it. When Echelon detects a key word or phrase it immediately puts a trace on the phone. It is also able to use any mobile phone as a tracking device enabling it to locate the user via their phone's 'cell ID'.

What has the end of the Cold War to do with this? The collapse of communism and the end of the Cold War freed up a vast reservoir of skilled manpower and spying technology. This happened at a time when there was an unprecedented revolution in information technology, the most prominent products of which were a new breed of satellites, the mobile phone, the Internet and developments in computer technology leading to the personal computer.

Echelon has the capacity to intercept 100,000 telephone calls at any one time.

What role do computers play in fighting crime? Without computers, dataveillance – which makes it possible to monitor larger and larger groups, including whole populations – would not be feasible. Dataveillance brings together surveillance techniques and enormous databases. The most obvious example is the matching of a facial image, captured by CCTV, with digitized images stored in a database, in order to identify a wanted criminal.

What has terrorism got to do with monitoring the whole population? Much of the technology was first used to monitor the IRA, which was at large among the general population. The government's first computerised database was used in Northern

Ireland to bring together information on terrorist suspects. In a similar way, events such as 7/7 indicate that Islamic terrorists are often indistinguishable from their host community. The introduction of a national ID card and the attempt to extend detention without charge of terrorist suspects for up to 42 days are two controversial aspects of the government's response to the terrorist threat.

Since the end of the terrorist threat in Northern Ireland, MI5 has increasingly sought to create a niche for itself in police surveillance work. In May 2000 the Sunday Times reported that MI5 was in the process of building a new £25 million surveillance centre capable of monitoring all email and internet messages sent or received in Britain. This is GTAC – the Government Technical Assistance Centre – housed in MI5's London headquarters and remodelled to act in support of the police.

The rise of Big Brother – the issues

From the 16th century the government has monitored those considered to be a threat to society.

It was only in 1841 that the government began to gather detailed information on everyone in the country.

As the 19th century progressed the police began to gather more detailed information on criminals and use technological advances to counter crime.

The Second World War led to an increase in government monitoring and national ID cards.

The government now uses technology developed in the Cold War to spy on its own people. The national ID card and powers of detention without charge introduce restrictions on civil liberties unparalleled in peacetime.

Who wants to know what we're doing?

Governments have gathered information about the population since they were able to keep records, primarily for taxation purposes. There are also powerful commercial interests with an insatiable appetite for personal information. Everyone who has something to sell – whether it's vitamins or a political opinion – believes that detailed information will improve their effectiveness. Throughout the 20th century the amount of information-gathering has increased exponentially. Pocket Issues asks how and why this has happened and how it affects our liberty.

Why has the government gathered so much more information on the population since 1900? As the 19th century progressed the government took on ever increasing responsibilities for the population, none of which could be met without the relevant information. For instance, the government could not provide appropriate education unless it knew the number, age, geographical distribution and requirements of children.

Since 1945, people have demanded improved public services and the government cannot supply them without ever more detailed information on the population. For instance, the demand for high quality health care is a major impetus to the development of the NHS database, currently estimated to have cost £31 billion, which will ensure that any doctor treating a patient has access to every detail of his medical history. This is merely one facet of the Labour government's aim to provide each citizen with a tailor-made package of services to suit his or her needs.

When did this information-gathering increase most? War and threats to national security have been the main spurs. All governments must protect its citizens against enemy attack, whether from air raids or spies. During the Second World War every adult was registered, issued with an identity card, obliged to report any change of address and was liable to conscription for war work.

In June 2008 Gordon Brown tried to extend detention without charge to 42 days.

But Britain has not been involved in a major war for sixty years.
No, but immediately after the end of the Second World War,
Britain and her allies became locked in a Cold War with the USSR
and faced the possibility of nuclear annihilation.

At the same time there were other threats:

The threat of terrorism: Terrorist threats – from Catholics,
Jacobites, French revolutionaries, anarchists, Bolsheviks and
Fenians – pre-date the 20th century. But when the IRA exploded
their first mainland bomb on 8 March 1973 the government
took unprecedented steps to counter them. Twenty years later,
when the Bishopsgate bomb exploded in the City (Square Mile)
and damaged the NatWest Tower, the government immediately
imposed a security ring around the area including concrete and
steel barriers manned by police who checked everyone entering
the City. Every building bristled with CCTV cameras, controlled
from a monitoring station in Bishopsgate police station, and
covering every millimetre of the City.

What about 9/11? The events of 9/11 in New York immediately
ratcheted security to even higher levels. The US government
introduced the Patriot Act, which undermined many rights and
freedoms. In Britain, Blair's Labour government followed suit
with restrictions on civil liberties and his successor, Gordon
Brown, subsequently tried to extend detention without charge to
42 days. Both countries are making massive investments in
information-gathering technology to counter state-aided sabotage
and track weapons of mass destruction.

Since October 2007 telecoms companies have been required
to keep records of phone calls and emails for 12 months. The
government's forthcoming Communications Data Bill will extend

this provision to cover Internet, email and voice-over-the-Internet use and necessitate increased monitoring by ISPs.

The threat of football hooliganism: In the 1980s Margaret Thatcher's government made football hooliganism the foremost public order issue. In 1985 the Football Trust provided grants to all football league clubs to establish surveillance systems in their grounds. The growth of shopping malls in the same decade acclimatised people to surveillance.

The ILOVEYOU virus proved the vulnerability of Britain's telecommunications infrastructure.

The threat of crime: Organised crime has become more sophisticated and technology-savvy. Economic globalisation, made possible by new communication technologies, allows multinational companies to do business instantaneously. But it also makes it possible for globally organised criminal networks to function.

Can crime take the form of internet sabotage? Yes. The vulnerability of Britain's telecommunications infrastructure to disruption was demonstrated in 2000 by the impact of the ILOVEYOU virus. A Filipino student, with cheap equipment, was able to cause world-wide disruption. In Britain it affected Parliament, Barclay's Bank, News International, the BBC and British Telecom. It cost billions of pounds.

To prevent a repetition of this it is argued that more surveillance of cyberspace is essential. The government cannot counter electronic money laundering, drug trafficking, arms trafficking, smuggling and the threat of hacking without intercepting communications. Similarly, the massive increase in economic and political migrants, together with the expansion of the EU, necessitates monitoring of the population in order to counter the operations of migrant criminals and illegal immigrants. It is this extent of crime that many feel makes blanket surveillance essential.

What about monitoring by ISPs to prevent crime? The powerful entertainment industry is putting immense pressure on ISPs to monitor the way their services are used to prevent the pirating of music and films. A Belgian copyright group has won a significant ruling against an ISP and Eircom, the major Irish provider, is being sued for failing to prevent users illegally sharing songs. The British government is keen that ISPs should face prosecution if they do not take strong action − similar to that recently enshrined in French law, whereby illegal use of the Internet results in disconnection − against users who make illegal downloads. All this is leading to more ISP monitoring of the individual's use of the Internet.

The threat of sexual predators: Paedophilia, child pornography and the stalking of children are crimes which greatly concern the public. These crimes are particularly associated with the Internet and demand some form of Internet surveillance.

The philosophy of crime prevention: Many criminologists argue that the extent of certain types of crime is such that only blanket surveillance can counter them. Car crime is a case in point. At any one time there are at least 8,500,000 cars on British roads that are either untaxed, uninsured, driven illegally or involved in crime. As fear of violent crime continues to spiral many politicians are convinced that blanket CCTV surveillance of public space is an effective antidote to public fears. Since the 1990s four-fifths of the Home Office anti-crime budget has been spent on CCTV.

How do businesses use personal data? They use it in targeted marketing, which is infinitely more cost-effective than scattergun advertising.

When did they start gathering our personal data? It began with the credit reference agencies in the 1950s, which became necessary with the growth of hire purchase. Today Britain's credit reference agencies hold as much personal information as the Police National Computer (PNC).

How has it developed? Information-gathering reached a new level with the junk mail revolution of the 1970s, which employed a scattergun technique. It began by using lists compiled from telephone directories before becoming far more focused in the 1990s. By then some written inducements to buy came printed with the householder's personal name, arrived on his birthday or contained personalised quotes. Since then marketing has become more sophisticated and consumer-specific, with direct mailing, telemarketing and Internet advertising carefully tailored to the target individual.

Personal information is an extremely valuable commodity.

What part does the Internet play? Though undoubtedly a fantastic resource for millions, the Internet has sparked a revolution in information-gathering. Businesses routinely collect and mine the personal data that consumers leave behind whenever they are online. When you sign up with a site you often have to provide a good deal of personal information which can then be analysed, assessed and – unless you take some steps to prevent it by 'opting out' – sold on to consumer-targeting operations. Such operations may then sell, trade, or share your information with third party companies, often without your knowledge or consent and sometimes to companies that send unsolicited commercial emails (spam). Some companies even mine email addresses from indirect sources, such as messages posted on mailing lists, newsgroups or domain name registration data.

Most of us also realise that we have to be wary of 'phishing' by fraudsters who send out emails, purportedly from legitimate financial institutions, in the hope that we will be tricked into using false websites to provide them with vital login information to access our bank accounts.

How else is information gathered? By tracking our consumer history. Every time you take out a loan, a HP agreement, a credit or loyalty card, buy a house or make any other significant financial transaction you reveal personal information and start to build up a credit rating. The largest of the credit reference agencies, Experian, has records on 45 million people in Britain – almost the entire adult population.

How do political parties use this information? It is now central to their election campaigns and was used by all three major parties in the 2005 general election. By analysing data on the electorate, much of it gleaned from loyalty card databases, they predict our concerns and thus are able to target and tailor their message. The Conservative Party has developed 'Voter Vault' and Labour 'Labour Contact.'

Why do so many companies and organisations feel it is necessary to keep their customers under surveillance?
80% of CCTV cameras are in the hands of private companies, which are trusted to operate them within a framework of self-regulation. Loss of confidence in the police and the criminal justice system has led many organisations to take responsibility for protecting themselves from crime. The increase in identity fraud, which costs the British economy £1.7 billion a year, has also spurred many businesses to monitor their customers with CCTV.

A spate of babies stolen from hospitals, the three-fold increase in attacks on health workers, teachers and people using public transport since the 1970s, combined with litigation against employers liable for not taking adequate measures to protect employees, have all fuelled the demand for improved security in the workplace. Incidents such as the Dunblane school shootings in 1996 continue to fuel public fears many years after the event and drive the demand for CCTV in and around schools.

Loss of confidence in the police has led many organisations to take responsibility for protecting themselves from crime.

Why do companies watch their employees? As long ago as 2001 84% of British companies admitted to some form of staff monitoring. Employers argue that they are compelled to do this because they are now expected to implement a bewildering raft of health and safety regulations and protect staff from violence. Companies also want to avoid falling victim to the ever-increasing opportunities for employee theft. As more companies develop a global, online existence, the potential for theft and industrial sabotage escalates.

So those are the justifiable reasons. Any less justifiable ones? Many companies have used these requirements as a pretext for invasive snooping. On 27 March 2008 The Guardian ran an article reporting that the discount supermarket chain Lidl, with more than 7,500 stores in 24 counties (including Britain) had been accused of spying on its employees, including keeping records of how many times they went to the toilet as well as details of their social lives and friends, their personal finances and female employees' menstrual cycle.

In January 2008 Microsoft filed a patent for new software that will monitor every facet of an employee's physiology.

In January 2008 Microsoft filed a patent for new software that will monitor every facet of an employee's physiology throughout the entire working day. Never mind that there is evidence that intrusive surveillance at work increases employee stress and destroys trust and staff morale.

Anything else? Employee abuse of the Internet is a major concern. Research shows many workers spend several working hours every day surfing personal interest sites, buying online or viewing pornography. Every day In Britain there are four million hits on child pornography sites – many by employees during working hours, using employers' computers.

The use of drugs? A recent case involving a large number of civil servants caught on CCTV taking drugs has led to greater surveillance in the workplace. Many industries now record all calls made from company telephones on the basis of consumer protection, security and training.

Who wants to know what we're doing – the issues

Governments have always gathered information on the population.

Today they do this so they can provide the services people demand and protect the population.

The government also has a responsibility to safeguard communication highways.

Many people believe mass surveillance provides the best way to counter crime.

ISPs are being required to monitor and censor use of the Internet.

Businesses want personal information so they can target advertising and increase sales.

Hire purchase and junk mailing stimulated the information-gathering industry.

The Internet has increased the personal data available to retailers.

Many companies, notably credit-rating agencies, make money by selling personal data.

Businesses monitor customers and staff in order to avoid theft, litigation, abuse of the Internet and drug use.

Why do people exchange private information?

Millions of people go online and reveal details about their personal lives, sexual activities, binge drinking and drug taking on a daily basis. While many others are more discreet, they nevertheless reveal to people they have never met things that they would not wish to become public knowledge. Yet this information is trawled, analysed and placed in databases which are sold to third parties, often without the knowledge or consent of the people they relate to. Pocket Issue asks some key questions.

How does this exchange of information happen? It is often the result of Internet based social networking sites. Last year there were an estimated 70 million sites online and their numbers are increasing at the rate of 120,000 every day. It's estimated that there are nearly 1 billion members of social networking sites worldwide.

How do these sites work? They are usually free to join. Most provide members with their own home page or profile, on which they post their photograph, basic personal information, their outlook and interests. But the key attraction is that members can link with each other as friends, which allows them to communicate and gives access to more private content (e.g. pictures, applications for sharing music, books, quizzes and gossip) on each other's site. Each member's friends are listed on their site, as well as any other groups or networks that they might have joined. It is very common for friends to communicate or chat by writing public messages in each others profile.

In 2007 there were 274 million social networking users and they are increasing at the rate of 120,000 every day.

Which are the major social networking sites and how many people use them? Social networking websites are used by millions and social networking is now a part of everyday life. MySpace and Facebook are the most widely used in North America; Bebo, MySpace, Skyrock Blog, Facebook and Hi5 in Europe, Orkut and Hi5 in South and Central America and Friendster and Orkut in Asia and the Pacific Islands. Other major sites include Photobucket, YouTube, Flickr and Friends Reunited.

In usage terms My Space is currently the biggest player with in the order of 100 million accounts. There are also many sites that focus on reuniting previous offline networks, often accused of attracting those interested in extra-marital affairs. Friendster has 30 million accounts and Classmates Online has 40 million.

Facebook is valued at $15 billion — more than the entire Ford motor corporation.

Why are these sites so valuable? These sites are massive personal data warehouses. They allow retailers to do 'hyper-marketing' — that is to target customers on the basis of detailed knowledge of each individual's interests and tastes. This is why Facebook for instance is valued at $15 billion — more than the entire Ford motor corporation.

What's the attraction of these sites? In the words of Chris Williams of The Register, a leading Sci/Tech site, social networking sites are nothing less than 'magical and life-affirming'. Ofcom's more sober assessment of their appeal suggests users derive great satisfaction from building a group of friends and browsing others' profiles. These sites decrease the cost of maintaining acquaintances. They provide an important social support role, especially for those who find face-to-face communication difficult.

Do they provide work opportunities? MySpace is used heavily by musicians to promote their music and related events. Artists famously 'found' on Myspace include Lily Allen and the Arctic Monkeys. Other sites are introducing some similar features. Bebo, for instance, is promoting music and has enrolled 100,000 bands in a six month period.

Why are so many people prepared to divulge so much personal information? Ofcom research identifies a category of users who are 'Attention Seekers'. They attract comments from others by posting outrageous photographs of themselves and writing provocative profiles, which often contain very detailed information about the user.

Research suggests that, in general, users of social networking sites give little thought to the possibility that others, including prospective employers, may have access to what they divulge. There are well-documented cases where people have lost jobs and college places as a result of things they have revealed online.

The Internet is a highly distributed and transparent technology.

What evidence is there that criminals are using these sites? Criminal gangs now favour the likes of Facebook and MySpace, rather than phishing for online banking information, as an easier means of stealing financial details. For example, members of networking sites may post their date of birth and mothers' maiden name on their profile – data that can then be used to bypass bank security and obtain account numbers. Customer data is sold via instant-message or internet forums that are live for only a few days or even hours. Bank account data and other personal details are offered for sale on the Internet for as little as £5. Credit card details are often sold in "bulk buy" bundles. In the first half of 2007, investigators found 50 card numbers on sale for just £20 and 500 numbers for only £100. Also offered for sale were full identities. The internet is a highly distributed and transparent technology.

Why do people exchange private information – the issues

There are 274 million users of social networking sites.

They enable people to contact others with similar interests and outlook.

They are so valuable because they are a mine of information for anyone wanting to target customers.

They also provide users with a valuable social support system.

Many users divulge personal information.

Criminals regard these sites as an easy source of financial details.

Do you know you're being watched?

For many people the most sinister aspect of surveillance is being spied on without knowing it. The prevalence of this covert monitoring of law-abiding people is a major contributor to the Big Brother society. Pocket Issue eavesdrops.

When are we likely to be spied on without knowing it or giving our consent?

In the workplace Surveys of global corporations and major businesses in the USA and UK indicate that up to 60% of the workforce is subject to some form of electronic surveillance, often imposed as a condition of employment with little legal protection.

Surveillance and monitoring have become design components of modern information systems and work environments. Modern network systems can interrogate computers and provide a profile of each user including their email and Internet use. The Computer Keyboard Monitoring System, developed by Britain's Vascom, transmits every keystroke to a receiver module, while Tech Assist Inc monitors everything an employee does on the computer. The Ascentor package even scrutinises a company's email traffic phrase by phrase.

The number of CCTVs in Britain increases by 20% every year.

In public areas Surveys show that 33% of people in Britain don't realise they are being watched in public places. Nor do they accept that those doing the watching can be "completely trusted to use it only for the public good." The number of CCTVs in Britain increases by 20% every year and they are now deployed in combination with new face recognition software, notably in the London Borough of Newham, to locate criminals.

When attending a football match Surveillance has led to the successful prosecution of hooligans and the solution to what once seemed the intractable problem of disorder at football matches. Consequently the filming of crowds at sporting events is now standard procedure.

When coming into contact with the police The UK has the largest DNA database in the world containing five percent of the population and hundreds of children under the age of ten. And not all those on the database are criminals The law was changed in 2001 to allow for the inclusion of samples from people who were not convicted and even from those never charged (except in Scotland). It was widened in 2003 to allow police to take a sample from anyone arrested, no matter how minor the offence. Since 2005 it includes a sample from everyone who dies.

The UK DNA database includes a sample from everyone who dies.

When we buy anything using a card or any form of credit Most people know nothing about credit reference agencies and are completely unaware that they are compiling files on us without our consent.

Worryingly, companies have no procedure for checking the accuracy of their own data, so even those who pay their bills may be refused credit for no valid reason. What's more, the credit details of people living at the same address are cross-referenced. The result of this is that all members of the household are tarred with the same brush as a single wayward payer. People living in rented accommodation or moving to premises with a poor credit history often suffer the consequences of earlier tenants' failings.

When we use the Internet or email Cookies are small pieces of data that can tell a website when someone is accessing it, enabling the site to recognise return users and personalise their experience. Since cookies can also record user behaviour they have been criticised for invading our privacy, being the starting point for gathering data which may – together with details of our Internet purchases – then be analysed and sold to retailers.

When we enter or leave the country Project Semaphore records everyone entering and leaving the UK. Its coverage will soon include the entire 40 million domestic plane and ferry journeys made annually.

Much traffic monitoring is done to raise revenue.

When we drive a car On average, a car travelling on a British motorway is filmed once every four minutes. Although the authorities often cite our safety, there is reason to believe much of this traffic monitoring is a revenue-raising device. Police authorities are encouraged to increase revenue from motoring fines since they get to keep some of it. Speed cameras are now appearing on straight country roads far from housing.

Many motoring organisations claim that a lot of monitoring is carried out in an underhand manner, with concealed cameras. What's more there is considerable evidence that the public is becoming increasingly resentful and alienated by what it sees as the targeting of the law-abiding citizen.

But don't these measures improve road safety? Some motoring organisations believe this over-reliance on electronic monitoring of traffic is leading to the under-policing of roads and a subsequent increase in dangerous driving – a major cause of accidents often undetected by these electronic devices.

Is observation of the motorist set to increase? Recent developments in transport-monitoring technology – such as Intelligent Road Studs and the Sureway Video Detection Device which can be used to take digital photographs of the front of a car which register the number plates and the driver and calculate the speed at which a vehicle is travelling – can be linked to the DVLA and automatically generate a fine. In areas where these devices have been trialled there has been an enormous increase in the number of fines issued. If the system were rolled out nationally it would result in 10 million fines a year.

At least this information is available only to the police? Licence plate data gathered by roadside cameras is also made available to foreign security services, as revealed by the Home Secretary to the House of Commons in April 2008. Personal information from government computers is regularly disclosed in error or for profit.

More than 200,000 illegal requests for information are made each year by private investigators.

For profit: The Information Commissioner's reports for 2006 exposed a growing illegal trade in personal information between police and private detectives. The Foundation for Information Policy Research (FIPR) estimates that more than 200,000 illegal requests for information are made each year by private investigators under false pretences.

In error: On a far larger scale, in November 2007, HMRC lost discs containing personal information on 25 million people – nearly half of Britain's population – including national insurance and bank account numbers. In January 2008 a Ministry of Defence laptop with the records of 600,000 recruits was stolen from a car in Birmingham. In both cases subsequent independent inquiries found security procedures 'woeful.' In the space of a few weeks in September 2008 the government lost the data of 130,000 offenders and more worryingly that of 5,000 employees of the National Offender Management Service.

Even the Police National Computer has 120,000 entry points and breaches are frequent. Once all databases are linked there will be countless access points to masses of information on everyone. Each access point poses a threat to data security.

Do errors like this put the government off gathering information? The government seems determined to press on with the creation of bigger and bigger databases. It recently announced its determination to create a massive database holding details of every phone call, email and the time spent on the Internet by every member of the public. ISPs and telecoms companies would gather this information and then hand it over to the Home Office. The government would require permission from the courts to access it.

Do you know you're being watched – the issues

Whether we're at work, walking or driving home, cheering on our local team or shopping, we are being watched.

The police are taking every opportunity to build up their DNA database.

Motorists are being increasingly hit as an easy source of revenue.

Police data is increasingly made available to people who have no right to it. Enormous databases are available to criminals because of appalling security lapses.

ISPs are increasingly required to monitor and record the activities of their customers and retain the data.

What are the dangers of government surveillance?

Many observers believe that the British public is tolerating a degree of government surveillance that was unthinkable even 30 years ago. They fear the present situation is fraught with danger. Pocket Issue finds out where the problems lie.

What are the major concerns? All data is fallible – mistakes occur at every stage of collection and processing. Consequently, people may be unjustly blacklisted as a result of information that does not have to be verified. Sensitive information may fall into criminal hands. For instance, in 2004 an animal rights extremist employed by the DVLA used details from the database to target staff at a guinea pig farm.

Information may be used for purposes that have nothing to do with why it was originally gathered. Information from the DNA database could prove family relationships, non-paternity and genetic tendencies to ill health that could be of use to drug and insurance companies.

Anyone prepared to pay can buy your personal data and use it for what ever purpose they choose.

Why is there so much concern about violation of the individual's right to privacy? There is now a massive international market in information. Data is being collected everywhere without our permission and without any real safeguards to prevent it from falling into the wrong hands. Despite the provisions of the Data Protection Act our personal data is supplied to a wide variety of people – thus reducing its security. Anyone prepared to pay for it can buy it and use it for what ever purposes – criminal or legal – they choose.

Why is there no effective regulation? Technological development is so rapid that it has left regulation trailing in its wake. For many areas there are not even established codes of practice let alone statute regulation. There are few court precedents.

Why do some people claim the government is using the threat of terrorism to undermine civil rights? The public tends to think that any restriction of our civil liberties is justified in countering terrorism. Politicians see this as an opportunity to extend their powers. The Prevention of Terrorism Act 2005 introduced control orders (restrictions on an individual suspect) that included allowing the Home Secretary to ban terrorist suspects from using the Internet and mobile phones, restrict their travel and prohibit association with named individuals. Suspects may be tagged and subject to house arrest or curfew. It applies to all British citizens and is regarded as illiberal because it removes the presumption of innocence.

Under current anti-terror laws you can be detained and questioned by police for up to 28 days without charge.

Under current anti-terror laws you can be detained and questioned by police for up to 28 days without charge. The government recently tried to extended this to 42 days in the face of fierce parliamentary opposition, including the resignation of the shadow Home Secretary, David Davis, in order to force a by-election on the issue. Neither the police nor the security services sought this increased power. The government eventually abandoned this measure in October 2008 but only after the House of Lords had rejected it.

When the threat of Islamic terrorism is defeated will the government still have grounds for using these powers? Powers assumed during emergencies are seldom relinquished when the threat passes. Instead they form a precedent for future breaches of human rights. The government's recent decision to detain Islamic extremists in Belmarsh prison without charge was made easier because it had done the same to terrorist suspects in the Maze prison in the 1970s, an internment camp in Northern Ireland. Likewise, six years after the Terrorism Act 2000 allowed police to stop and search any person or vehicle in designated areas, it has been used on 22,672 occasions. Civil liberties groups feel that such frequency of use indicates that these powers are not being used as envisaged by the original legislation. The restrictions on these powers are so weak that they have even been used to prevent peaceful and democratic protest.

Are such powers necessary to protect the public from dangerous subversives? Many civil liberties groups are concerned that the definition of 'subversive' has changed in a sinister way. From referring to someone who seeks to overthrow the government by unlawful, usually violent means, it has come to refer to anyone who challenges social norms, even if they do this by legitimate, legal or democratic means. Identifying those who pose a threat to society is increasingly a matter of discretion by unaccountable officials. In 2005, police used the Terrorism Act to arrest an 82-year-old man who heckled Jack Straw at the Labour Party conference.

What evidence is there that legal, democratic organisations are targeted for surveillance? During the post-war era MI5's F branch, responsible for domestic intelligence, has developed greatly. Its sub-section FX ran investigations into trade unions and monitored prominent figures such as Arthur Scargill and Mick McGaghey together with leftist politicians such as Tony Benn and Ken Livingstone. In 1983 the Ministry of Defence created a clandestine section DS19 to monitor CND, whose offices it subsequently bugged. The Campaign's front man, Bruce Kent, was the subject of constant monitoring. An informer was planted in his office.

But this was all a long time ago. More recently at least two members of the present Labour government attracted the unwanted attention of the security services. Patricia Hewitt was general secretary of the National Council for Civil Liberties and Harriet Harman one of its legal advisers. Both successfully sued the government in the European Court of Human Rights.

Where do the proposed ID cards fit into this? Many civil liberties organisations feel they will make matters worse. They will enable the government to record the movements of every citizen and this information will be stored in databanks run by private security companies. As technology improves and the various databases are linked the government will have details of our health, credit rating, holidays abroad, voting and everything else that requires us to present some sort of identification.

The UK is "sleepwalking into a surveillance society."

Why don't people trust the government to use this information properly? All intelligence data, whether it relates to the civil population or other states, is subject to abuse. The Anglo-American invasion of Iraq was justified on the grounds that that there were weapons of mass destruction ready to launch an attack on Britain within an hour. After the invasion the British government was forced to admit that no such threat existed. Also the government has regularly shown itself to be incredibly careless with large amounts of sensitive data.

Does this amount to a threat to democratic freedoms – are we drifting into a Big Brother society? Monitoring agencies think so. Britain's Information Commissioner has warned that the UK is "sleepwalking into a surveillance society." Privacy International's comparative study found that surveillance permeates every facet of British society, that the situation here is worse than in any other EU country and at the same level as in Russia, China and Singapore. Britain is an enthusiastic world leader in adopting intrusive surveillance technologies such as biometrics, digital CCTV, computer databases and DNA testing, all of which have been implemented with little debate. And it's getting worse.

What reasons are there for thinking the situation is about to get worse? In order to establish its credentials as tough on crime and terrorism the present Labour government has enacted an avalanche of new laws limiting human rights, including freedom of assembly, privacy, freedom of movement, the right to remain silent when arrested and freedom of speech.

What are the dangers of government surveillance – the issues

The volume of information gathered means many mistakes are inevitable.

Lack of effective regulation means serious violations of the individual's right to privacy occur.

The government is using the threat of terrorism to undermine everyone's liberties.

Those who question government policy may be targeted as a subversive.

ID cards will only increase this threat to individual liberties.

The government already has us all under surveillance and plans to increase its grip.

Changing attitudes to a surveillance society

Both the government and the public have become convinced that threats to national and personal security justify encroachment on civil liberties and personal privacy rights. Yet what is tolerated today would have aroused fierce opposition 30 years ago. Similarly, advances in retail technology and increased use of credit and loyalty cards together with Internet shopping have made it possible to build up comprehensive customer profiles on every one of us. The public is generally apathetic to these developments. Pocket Issue looks at the facts behind the attitude.

When did these changes begin? It is difficult to specify the date when this change started but many commentators believe it is closely linked to the threat of terrorism. The reality of the threat began to dawn on the British public only on 8 March 1973 with the explosion of the first IRA bomb on the mainland, outside the Army Recruiting Office in Great Scotland Yard. This was the beginning of a series of mainland attacks that threatened the lives and property of the whole population.

We have already entered a new era of pre-emptive policing.

More recently this fear has been replaced by the fear of Islamic terrorists who may have access to explosives, poisons and chemicals that could threaten large swathes of the population. Many would argue that we have already entered a new era of pre-emptive policing. Law enforcement and intelligence agencies cannot afford to wait until terrorists blow up our cities or kill hundreds of civilians. They must take pre-emptive action and this involves conducting mass surveillance of the general population in order to identify potential threats.

What about fear of crime? Parallel to the growing terrorist threat has been a steadily increasing fear of crime among all sections of the population. Organisations working with the elderly suggest that this fear effectively confines many people to their homes after dark. A government report released in June 2008 showed that 25% of British children live in fear of crime. In reality neither of these are most likely to be victims of violent crime. That unhappy distinction belongs to young men. A Global Attitudes project shows that 69% of Britons are 'seriously worried about crime.'

The accessibility of child pornography and Internet fraud are major worries.

What about the role of the Internet? The problems of unregulated communication are becoming more and more evident. The accessibility of child pornography and Internet fraud are major worries, as is the use of the Internet by paedophiles to groom victims. The abduction or murder of children quite rightly commands blanket media coverage.

Why are these developments significant? The public demands that the police take action to track down and eliminate the threat of these criminals before they strike. Consequently, the British public is remarkably uncritical of developments in surveillance. Most surveys show that the concerns of civil liberties groups are not reflected in the wider population.

Changing attitudes to a surveillance society – the issues

Fear of terrorism makes the public receptive to mass surveillance.

Fear of crime seems to make increased surveillance justifiable.

Fear of paedophiles is widespread and their activities are strongly linked with the Internet in the public mind.

The public demands protection from terrorists and criminals and is little concerned about this impinging on civil liberties.

Civil liberties – safeguards and threats

The major safeguards of our civil liberties are legislation and the monitoring bodies. However, critics point out that both have limited powers and fail to provide effective sanctions against those who threaten our privacy. Expressions of concern about the extent and use of surveillance in Britain are now a daily occurrence. In its report on ID cards the Commons home affairs committee expressed its fear that the cards might be used for surveillance as part of "function creep". By this they mean the use of data collected for one reason being used for another. Realistic given that the police currently use information from loyalty cards and London's Oyster travel cards to track people's movements. Pocket Issue sticks its oar in the water.

Which laws protect the individual's right to privacy? There are two types of law that do this: international and domestic. Article 12 of the Universal Declaration of Human Rights states that "No one shall be subjected to arbitrary interference with his privacy." Article 8 of the European Convention on Human Rights reaffirms this right and was incorporated into UK law by the Human Rights Act 1998 (HRA).

What privacy rights do these laws guarantee? These laws create a general right to privacy, which did not previously exist in law. Article 8 offers general protection for a person's private and family life, home and correspondence, from unjustified State interference.

The government may be justified in interfering with our privacy.

Does this mean that no one has any right to violate our privacy? No. Our right to privacy is qualified. Under certain circumstances the government may be justified in interfering with our privacy.

What exactly are these circumstances? First, the interference must be justified, for instance in terms of safeguarding national security. Further, any interference must be in accordance with the law, in accordance with Article 8 and necessary in a democratic society. However, many argue that the right to privacy bestowed by these laws is too general and therefore easy for the government to get around in practice. What makes this likely is the tendency of the courts to take a very narrow view of privacy.

What's more worrying is that these laws are generally taken by the courts to refer only to individual privacy and do little to regulate or restrict surveillance.

Do these same conditions apply to individuals, as opposed to the government, who might want to interfere with our privacy?
The legal situation is not entirely clear, as there is no general right of privacy from interference by individuals. However, the right to respect for privacy under Article 8, together with protections provided by common law, and the new obligation on courts to interpret statutory law wherever possible in a way which is consistent with Convention rights, should go some way to protecting against the invasion of privacy in practice. But this will only become clear as courts make decisions on these cases and precedent is built up.

We have the right to see all information about us that has been recorded anywhere by public or private organisations.

What about information that has been gathered legally or with our permission: is there a law allowing us to check that it is correct and that it is not used in ways we don't like?
The Data Protection Act is intended to do this. The UK Parliament approved the Data Protection Act in July 1998 to implement the European Union Data Protection Directive. It covers any personal information regardless of how it is stored, on a computer database or on paper files. The Law applies to information held

by both government agencies and private entities. It creates eight data protection principles. These provide for limitations on the use of personal information, access to, and correction of, records and adequate security. They require entities that maintain records to register with the Information Commissioner.

How is this law supposed to work? Take the Internet, for instance. Whenever personal data is entered on a website the website is legally bound to inform you what it is using it for and must also give you the option of barring them from passing it on to anyone else. Commercial organisations must only use the information given to them for the purposes stated in the agreement.

What about our right to check information held on us? Each of us has the right to see all information about us that has been recorded anywhere by public or private organisations. As an employee, you have the right to know about information obtained through surveillance. Your request for this information must be answered within forty days.

How else do these laws help us? They require commercial companies to justify retaining personal data or else delete it. There is a code of practice attached to the Act and the individual has recourse to law if he feels his rights have been impinged. The Act sets out certain basic standards: the data recorded on CCTV must be fairly and lawfully processed for limited purposes, must be adequate but relevant, accurate, not stored for longer than is necessary and should be processed in accordance with the individual's rights. It must be kept secure and must never be transferred to countries which do not provide adequate protection under the law. The law controls to whom the information may be revealed.

What can we do if we feel the government or a company are not doing this? The Act has a Data Commissioner to enforce it. The Commissioner can issue Enforcement Notices if he considers there has been a breach of the Act. But he has few investigatory powers and few sanctions.

The EU has recently introduced the office of European Data Protection Supervisor.

Critics, however, point out the short-comings of this law: there are many general exemptions, on the grounds of national security, law enforcement and the collection of taxes which in effect render it useless in protecting us against the state. The Act in no way restricts the gathering of personal information nor does it prevent it being passed on to others without our knowledge or consent. The EU has recently introduced the office of European Data Protection Supervisor (EDPS) which, like its British counterpart, focuses on individual data protection but has few powers with which to enforce its recommendations.

Are there any other relevant laws? The other major laws are the Freedom of Information Act (2000) and the Environmental Information Regulations Act (2004). They allow access to information from public and some private bodies. In total these laws covers more than 100,000 entities from your GP to the Ministry of Defence.

What rights do these Acts give us? The Freedom of Information Act gives you the right to see information held on you by public and other bodies. It also provides access to information about the way we are governed and the natural and commercial environment in which we live. Anyone making a request for information to a public authority is entitled to be informed in writing whether the authority has the information. If so, the person making the request is entitled to be given that information.

These laws are designed to bring about a change in the culture of government. In the words of Jack Straw, the Home Secretary who introduced them, they signified a shift in the default mode of the public services from 'this should be kept quiet unless…' to 'this should be published unless…' It creates, for the bodies covered by the Acts, a 'duty to confirm or deny.'

In 2004-5 the police used PACE to stop and search 851,200 people and vehicles.

How Does the Police and Criminal Evidence Act (PACE) affect our privacy rights? By the terms of this Act, passed in 1984, the police have the right to stop and search any person on the street on the grounds of suspicion. In 2004-5 the police used the Act to stop and search 851,200 people and vehicles in England and Wales. This was up 14% from the previous year. It also allows police to enter and search homes without a warrant following an arrest for any offence.

What has the Security Service Act got to do with this? The Security Service Act (last amended in 1996) regulates the way the security services operate. The Act provides for an oversight commissioner and a tribunal to investigate complaints against the service. However, many people believe both are toothless.

What safeguards are there for the law-abiding citizen against the wrongful application of the Prevention of Terrorism Act? The Home Secretary must apply to a High Court judge to make a control order. The Home Secretary's powers are temporary and relapse unless confirmed annually by Parliament. There is an independent reviewer who reports to Parliament on the Act and the use of control orders.

What is the Regulation of Investigatory Powers Act about? RIPA, passed in 2000, allows for the interception of telephone calls by the appropriate authorities – for example, the Security Service, the Secret Intelligence Service, NCIS, GCHQ, the Police and Customs – when the Home Secretary issues an interception warrant. This must name or describe either one person as the interception subject, or a single set of premises where the interception is to take place. In limited circumstances the Home Secretary may issue a 'certified' interception warrant which can disapply some of the requirements of a normal warrant and, in particular, the requirement to specify a person or premises.

Why is this Act so controversial? Many critics believe that this Act is in direct conflict with the Data Protection Act and in breach of the European Convention of Human Rights, which guarantees a right to privacy. RIPA makes it an offence for any person intentionally, and without lawful authority, to intercept any communication in the course of its transmission through a public telecommunication system and – except in specified circumstances – through a private telecommunication system.

However, the same Act gives the government access to any information on the grounds of 'national security, preventing or detecting crime, preventing disorder, public safety, protecting public health or the economic well-being of the UK.' Many argue that these grounds are so wide that they put an end to individual privacy. Even the flimsy legal restrictions stated in the Act are worth less than they might suggest. In 2007 the Home Secretary sanctioned the right of a host of government departments and local authorities to scrutinise an individual's private telephone records.

What are the shortcomings in the legislation designed to protect the rights of the public? Under the Prevention of Terrorism Act the Home Secretary is theoretically required to apply to a High Court judge to make a control order. However, he may decide to circumvent the application and refer it to the court for confirmation after the event.

What about gaps in the legislation? The Data Protection Act does not cover three major areas of surveillance. These are the use of surveillance by employers to ensure employees are complying with the terms of their contract of employment; security equipment installed by householders for home security purposes and cameras and similar equipment used by broadcast media for journalistic, artistic or literary purposes. What's worse, major organisations such as TFL admit to procedures which are contrary to the DPA, such as failure to tell consumers what personal information they are collecting and how it will be used.

What about exemptions? The Security Service (MI5), the Secret

Intelligence Service (MI6) and GCHQ all have an absolute exemption from the Freedom of Information Act. Though the Ministry of Defence and the Special Branch come under the Freedom of Information Act, any information they receive from the security service does not. A certificate from a minister is all that is required for the exemption to apply. Many argue that the exemption of the security services is particularly bad since many of the major scandals that led to the FOIA involved these services, such as the Matrix-Churchill arms-to-Iraq case in 1992.

What about the monitoring agencies? Unlike the USA where powerful Congressional committees keep the security services constantly accountable to the people's democratically elected representatives, Britain has only token oversight. The Intelligence and Security Services Committee cannot monitor the agencies' operations or enquire into their work practices and systems. Under the Security Services Act the commissioner can only investigate the agency if a successful complaint has been made. Only 2% of complaints are deemed worthy of investigation.

What about the Regulator appointed under the Freedom of Information Act? The Regulator, Richard Thomas, has so far not used the sanctions at his disposal when the government has failed to comply with the Act. Many feel that there are too many exceptions to the provisions of the Act. A large part of the Act is taken up with details of all those who are exempt.

"You have zero privacy anyway. Get over it." Scott McNealy, CEO of Sun Microsystems.

What about controls over the technology of surveillance? In Britain there is no law against the sale or purchase of the most sophisticated bugging equipment – it is simply illegal to use it. Thousands of products come on the market every year, many originally developed for military use. Among these are image and sound amplification devices, infra-red binoculars, light amplifiers, satellite cameras, directional microphones, image and sound recording devices, miniature video cameras and parabolic microphones to detect conversations over a kilometre away. Lorraine Electronics' multi-room surveillance system DIAL (Direct Intelligence Access Listening) enables the operator to monitor several rooms in a building from anywhere in the world. A specially programmed laptop can capture all the mobile phones and cordless phones active within an area. Spying technology is widely used by the media to gather information on people in the public eye.

In reality there is nothing to stop any organisation or individual from acquiring this technology and using it to invade the privacy of any individual they target. The attitude of big business is perhaps best expressed by Scott McNealy, CEO of Sun Microsystems. In his words, "You have zero privacy anyway. Get over it."

Civil liberties: safeguards and threats – the issues

Our right to privacy is enshrined in both international and national laws. But this right is so general that it is easy for the government to get round it.

Our rights against individuals invading our privacy are unclear.

The Data Protection Act is supposed to safeguard information about us and ensure we have the right to check its accuracy.

The Freedom of Information Act provides public access to information held by public and private bodies.

PACE gives the police unlimited powers to stop and search.

The Security Services Act gives the Home Secretary the power to impose control orders.

Those organisations most likely to spy on the public are exempt from the Freedom of Information Act.

The Regulator is toothless.

Anyone who can afford the technology can violate our privacy, although illegally.

The key players

The key players

Who are the people and institutions that affect our liberties and privacy? From government through to internet companies, Pocket Issue compiles a list.

Government and security services

The British government seems inextricably locked into the culture of surveillance and data gathering. It sees both as key to countering the threat of crime and terrorism and believes that detailed information on the population is essential to meet public demand for services and amenities.

Government Agencies The Inland Revenue, the DVLA, the Department of Social Security, the Police National Computer, the Crown Prosecution Database and public utilities now have a vast amount of information on us all. The government is working towards bringing all this information together.

The Police The Serious and Organised Crimes Agency, for instance, at the forefront of the fight against drug trafficking and money laundering, routinely mines hundreds of linked databases, containing billions of bank transactions, the majority of which are perfectly innocent.

The US government Britain and the USA cooperate so closely on intelligence gathering that developments in one inevitably affect the other. The Pentagon's Total Information Awareness programme, which mines data on its citizens in order to detect suspicious patterns of behaviour that might indicate terrorist intent, continues apace despite Congressional efforts to halt it. TIA has a British equivalent. Microsoft's recent purchase of the Norwegian company FAST, a leader in data mining on behalf of governments, suggests that expertise in this area is increasingly concentrated in American hands.

Business

Big Business Gathering and processing information on consumers is an expanding business, constantly increasing in scope and value. In a competitive marketplace no retailing organisation can afford to ignore this resource.

Dotcom Companies The growth of social networking remains remarkable. In a recent report, Ofcom described social networking as now "mainstream communications technology for many people." Their research shows that 22% of Internet users over the age of 16 and 49% of children over the age of eight have set up a profile on a social networking site. The information they provide is incredibly valuable. It is in part what lies behind the astronomical stock market valuations of many dotcom companies.

Employers Common surveillance includes videotaping all areas of the workspace, including toilets and workstations and the use of covert cameras to monitor employee performance. Smart ID cards which track the employee's movements around a building are becoming common. Over and above the routine recording and monitoring of all phone calls, many companies are employing TMS telephone analysis. BT call centre employees are regularly confronted with an evaluation of their work relative to that of other workers. Systems such as Trackback monitors mobile workers and tell management a vehicle's exact location at all times.

European justice

The European Court of Human Rights Though the Human Rights Act is in force in the UK it is still possible to make an application to the European Court. However, three requirements must first be met and these make appealing to the Court a last resort.

What are these requirements? Firstly, you must feel that your rights under one or more of the articles of the Convention of Human Rights have been violated. Secondly, you must pursue any legal remedy available in the UK. In practice this means that you have taken the matter through the British courts. Finally, you must make your application to the European Court within six months of the conclusion of any court proceedings that you have taken in the UK or, if there were no proceedings that it was reasonable to expect you to take, within six months of the event which gives rise to your application.

How does a plaintiff apply to ECHR? It is possible to apply to the Court personally, but no one recommends this. A lawyer with relevant experience is obviously a great asset and far more likely to achieve a positive outcome than a layman. This expertise is especially important in the early stages of an application where most cases are deemed inadmissible. Even if a layperson did manage to negotiate the early stages without a lawyer and the Court decided to hold a hearing, the rules normally require that subsequently the plaintiff be represented by a lawyer.

Is public funding available? Yes. The problem is that the payments a lawyer receives under the scheme are very low. Lawyers experienced in international law generally command high fees.

British justice

The British Courts Anyone who believes that a public body such as the police, a government department or a local authority has acted in violation of his or her human rights may be able to challenge its action by taking judicial review proceedings in the High Court. If successful, the public body can be prevented from continuing to act unlawfully. The court can also reverse a decision made by a public body or make it reconsider that decision. Damages may be available in certain circumstances.

What are the difficulties? Judicial review is a complicated and costly process, though public funding is available. There is also a time limit: the review must be initiated within three months of the decision being challenged. Court proceedings should be a last resort, considered only when every other avenue of redress has been pursued.

What should an aggrieved person do before considering court action? The first step is to find out if there is a person designated to deal with complaints, perhaps someone appointed under the relevant legislation. These people include:

a) The Information Commissioner The Data Protection Act allows individuals to see information held about them and to correct it if it is wrong. Organisations that hold our personal information must use it fairly, keep it secure, make sure the information is accurate and keep it up to date.

The Act also gives individuals the right to stop their personal information being used for unwanted marketing. The Privacy and Electronic Communications Regulations give us the right to stop electronic direct-marketing messages including phone calls, faxes, emails and texts.

If an individual thinks an organisation may have breached the Data Protection Act in the way it holds and handles his or her personal information, they may complain to the Information Commissioner's Office. Advice on how to complain is available at www.ico.gov.uk.

b) The Information Tribunal (formerly the Data Protection Tribunal) RIPA imposes a statutory duty of confidentiality on the police, civil servants and postal and telecommunication workers to keep secret the contents of any interception warrant, the details of its issue and implementation and everything in the intercepted material. It is therefore an offence to give disclosure of any of this. Further details on how to appeal against a disclosure are on the website at www.informationtribunal.gov.uk.

What if an aggrieved person is not happy with their decision? The next step is to seek legal advice.

Does the person seeking redress have to pay? Free legal advice is available from Law Centres and solicitors who offer a free initial interview, usually lasting 30 minutes.

Public Funding is available through the Community Legal Services fund (CLS, see Glossary). All the relevant information is available at: www.clsdirect.org.uk.

Public Funding to cover the cost of advice from a solicitor and having him write letters may also be available. This is known as 'Legal Help'. Applicants may also be entitled to Public Funding for a solicitor and/or barrister to represent them in court. For this a 'Legal Representation Certificate' is required. A solicitor must apply for this on behalf of his client.

What if the aggrieved person has difficulty getting representation? Some organisations such as the Bar Pro Bono Unit and the Free Representation Unit do provide free representation in some cases.

Should an aggrieved person seek legal help as a first resort? No. A lawyer in general practice is probably not the best starting point. There are a number of voluntary agencies that specialise in specific areas and each offers a wealth of expertise.

Other monitoring bodies

GeneWatch GeneWatch UK is a not-for-profit group that monitors developments in genetic technologies from a public interest, environmental protection and animal welfare perspective. GeneWatch believes people should have a voice in whether or how these technologies are used and campaigns for safeguards. It works on all aspects of genetic technologies.

Statewatch Comprises lawyers, academics, journalists, researchers and community activists. It encourages the publication of investigative journalism and critical research in Europe in relation to the state, justice and home affairs, civil liberties, accountability and openness. One of Statewatch's primary purposes is to encourage informed discussion and debate through the provision of news, features and analyses.

Liberty Liberty is also known as the National Council for Civil Liberties. Since its foundation in 1934 it has sought to safeguard fundamental rights and freedoms in England and Wales. It promotes the values of individual human dignity, equal treatment and fairness as the foundations of a democratic society. Liberty campaigns to protect basic rights and freedoms through the courts, in Parliament and in the wider community. It works through a combination of public campaigning, test case litigation, parliamentary lobbying, policy analysis and the provision of free advice and information.

Privacy International Privacy International (PI) is a human rights group formed as a watchdog on surveillance and privacy invasions by governments and corporations. It has campaigned across the world to protect people against intrusion by governments and corporations that seek to erode people's right to privacy. It strongly believes that privacy forms part of the bedrock of freedoms, and its goal is to preserve it.

Local Authorities More complaints and requests for information relate to local authorities than any other public body, which is hardly surprising given the scope of their activities. As an initial step it is generally better for an aggrieved person to deal directly with the service concerned, expressing their concerns directly to the relevant service. If they feel unable to do this, they should seek the help of their local councillor. Liaising between the local electorate and the local authority is something councillors are particularly well placed to do.

Members of Parliament If further help is required the local MP is a valuable resource. MPs provide help to all their constituents, regardless of political allegiance. The House of Commons Information Office provides the names of all MPs. It is also possible to contact them through their local constituency offices. Addresses and contact numbers are also available in local libraries, town halls, and the MP's personal website.
When writing to any MP the address to use is: House of Commons London SW1A 0AA. A letter allows the aggrieved

person to explain himself clearly and provides the MP with a record of the problem.

Stargazing

The good and the bad come 2020

Until recently it seemed that Britain was sleepwalking into a surveillance society. Almost without comment the British people have allowed government and business to intrude on every facet of life. However, people are belatedly waking up to the threat to individual liberty and the right to privacy. But is it too late to turn back the tide? Pocket Issue paints a good and bad picture come the year 2020.

The good

All commentators agree that an awareness of the seriousness of the threat to our liberties is the key to protecting them. Prominent public figures have been raising public consciousness and as a result more people are standing up against the Big Brother "creep". Informed opinion is becoming aware of the negative effects of over-regulation and monitoring. The think tank Civitas claims that child protection legislation and its resultant culture of suspicion is poisoning relationships between adults and children.

Slowly this is alerting the public to the dangers of Big Brother. Some observers suggest a parallel with global warming, for a long time a minority concern, now something that should become an international preoccupation.

The roll out of ID cards for every citizen leads to the largest march on Downing Street since the Poll Tax riots, and soon afterwards the incoming Tory party reverses the decision and withdraws them pending a full review. The few that had been issued become collectors items. With consecutive Governments fighting a number of real problems on other fronts including spiralling inflation, a C-difficile pandemic and unacceptable levels of unemployment, ministers have been too busy and possibly already too unpopular to risk resurrecting the issue. Meanwhile, anti terror laws have been tightened, making it harder for local councils to abuse them. Internet chat forums are approached with caution as people become increasingly aware of the opportunity they provide for identity fraud activity. Employees have been given a right to privacy at work in certain areas. Psychiatrists have recognised privacy invasion as a 21st century condition that can result in a nervous breakdown. "Feeling like you're being watched is no longer an indication of paranoia" announced a leading consultant.

With Civil liberties pressure groups working hard to keep the issue of privacy in the public's awareness, it would seem society is finding a new balance of what is acceptable in Big Brother terms, and what is not. While they accept that the government's powers are the most justifiable and so the most difficult to rein in, being photographed and fined for going two miles over the speed limit is now deemed a revenue raising joke at their expense. Overall, not perfect, but not Orwellian yet, either.

The bad

The public remain unconvinced about the extent of our Big Brother society. Many people ask, quite reasonably, 'If the government's power of surveillance is so comprehensive, why is it that a third of the prison population – surely the most intensely monitored people in the country – are regular users of illicit drugs? Why is it that, according to the government's own figures, there are at least 500,000 illegal immigrants living in Britain and over eight million cars on the road which are being driven illegally or involved in crime?'

Equally significant is the public's increasing fear of crime increases. Both the government and business see technology as the answer. Hidden mini cameras are appearing in buses, stations, telephone booths, public toilets, cinemas, shops and ATMs. Passive Millimetre Wave Imagers, cameras that can detect items concealed under people's clothes, are now being trialled at railway stations around England.

In parallel with this is the spiralling cost of identity fraud, particularly benefit fraud which remains a major drain on public resources. Personal Identification Verification systems are becoming big business and affecting all of us. Concern about illegal immigrants, especially criminals, continues to grow, helping to push through the concept of identity cards. Everyone is fingerprinted routinely, including babies at birth.

National ID cards are introduced. Similar in size to a credit card, this contains a photograph, iris scans, fingerprints or other biometrics. Initially compulsory for foreign nationals and 'high risk workers' it is soon extended to students and by 2011 to the rest of the population.

Meanwhile, the great surveillance juggernaut rolls on, its path smoothed by public complacency. MI5 recruits a further 1,500 employees and the government plans to give personal details of pensioners and poorer families to private energy firms.

A programme being developed by the EU to prevent terrorist attacks involves in-flight monitoring of passengers with tiny microphones and cameras installed in each passenger's seat and linked to computers which will constantly analyse facial expressions and conversations. Suspicious behaviour triggers an alarm.

Commercial pressure is working in the same direction. As early as June 2009 retailers at Portsmouth's Gunwarf Quays shopping complex pioneer a system of tracking shoppers' movements through their mobile phone signals. This enabled managers to identify the type of goods shoppers showed interest in, how long they stayed in the complex and even when they used the toilet. In the light of such developments, fictional depictions of the future – such as the film Minority Report in which Tom Cruise's biometric implants allow the shopkeeper to recall what he last bought – don't seem so fanciful.

Everything suggests that the government's and big business's insatiable appetite for information is advancing in tandem with the development of technology which is rapidly making Orwell's nightmare a reality.

What can you do?

How you can make a mark

What can you do?

You and your personal details are the raw material of dataveillance. There are many ways in which you can make a stand against encroachments on your privacy and the abuse of your personal data. Here are some simple steps to help you in the fight to keep some things private.

Personal information – protecting yourself against ID fraud.

When disposing of documents that show your name, address or other personal details, shred or burn them.

Always check bank and credit-card statements to ensure all transactions are legitimate.

Check your personal credit file regularly to ensure no one has used your name to apply for credit. (See Further Reading for more on this)

Ensure your home computer is protected before you go online. Install an effective anti-virus, firewall and anti-spam software package to guard against viruses and spyware which can be used to obtain your personal information.

Contact CIFAS – The UK's Fraud Prevention Service – to apply for protective registration. CIFAS will carry out extra checks to see when anyone, including you, applies for a financial service, such as a loan, using your address.

Make sure your operating system, usually a version of Microsoft Windows, is up to date. Windows Vista, the most recent, is more secure than its predecessors. Make sure your system is configured to automatically download updates.

First step: Treat your personal information as you would other valuables. Store all documents used to establish your identity – not just your passport and driving licence but also bank statements and utility bills – in a safe place.

Know your rights. You have the right to access information that organisations hold about you. Asking for your information is known as making a 'subject access request'. To do this, write or email the organisation you believe has information about you. Address your request to the company secretary.

Make sure your request includes your full name and address, including your postcode and any information that will help the organization to find your information and check that you are who you say you are. State in your request that you are asking for this information in accordance with your rights under the Data Protection Act.

Send your request by recorded delivery and keep a copy of the letter and any further letters you send or receive. The organization may ask for a small fee and is required to reply within 40 days.

If you still don't receive a reply, visit www.ico.gov.uk for advice on what to do next. Under the Data Protection Act you can demand to see your credit rating but the company is entitled to charge a fee. The two main companies are Experian, www.experian.co.uk, and Equifax, www.equifax.co.uk. For more information on this, visit www.ico.gov.uk to request a free copy of 'Credit explained'.

First step: Check your credit rating using the websites above.
Use Voluntary Organisations. There are a number of organisations which monitor encroachments on civil liberties and seek to protect the improper use of personal data. Liberty

and Privacy International are foremost among these. You can keep abreast of developments by checking their website. You may feel you want to support their campaigns.

First step: Check out the website of one of the voluntary organisations listed in Further Reading. They outline current issues.

Prevent Further Encroachment. Privacy Impact Assessment (PIA) is required in both the USA and Canada for all federal and public sector projects where personal data is processed. The UK government has shown some interest and should be pressurised to follow suit.

Use cash and snail mail – they prevent organisations from tracking your purchases and building up a customer profile.

Among the worst offenders are companies offering a warranty on goods you purchase. Many claim that in order to get the warranty to which you are legally entitled you have to complete and return a registration form. This is incorrect. They simply want you to provide them with a lot of personal information. All you need do to ensure your rights under retail legislation is retain the registration form together with the relevant receipt.

First step: Refuse to supply personal information unless you are satisfied with how it will be used.

Further reading

The best places to keep up-to-date

Further reading

Hopefully this Pocket Issue has given you a clearer idea of the issues surrounding Big Brother. You can keep in touch with the issue through our blog: http://blog.pocketissue.com

But we don't presume to offer the last word on this important and evolving subject, so here are some useful websites and books sourced to research this guide.

Protecting yourself against ID fraud

CIFAS is the UK's fraud prevention service at www.cifas.org.uk. Their site has lots of valuable information on how to avoid becoming the victim of fraud.

The FOIA Centre is a specialist, London-based, research company and consultancy which helps the public to use the Freedom of Information Act, www.foiacentre.com.

Keeping up-to-date

The mainstream media devotes little space to coverage and analysis of developments in this area. However, the BBC, www.bbc.co.uk, and The Guardian, www.guardian.co.uk, generally address these issues in a considered manner.

Official rulings

The Information Commissioner's site, www.informationtribunal. com, provides coverage of issues under consideration and related developments. The organisation of the site is clear and the language comprehensible.

The Activists

Privacy International campaigns across the world to protect people against intrusion by governments and corporations that seek to erode privacy. Its site, www.privacyinternational.org, is up-to-the-minute and extremely lucid.

Liberty is dedicated to protecting civil liberties and human rights, www.liberty-human-rights.org.uk. It provides detailed coverage of developments in this area and is a mine of information for anyone seeking help.

Statewatch monitors the state and civil liberties in Europe, www.statewatch.org. It offers advice and help to those with concerns and provides a forum for informed discussion on developments affecting civil liberties.

For the latest on developments in genetic technology and their impact on civil liberties see the GeneWatch site at www.genewatch.org.

Not forgetting Nineteen Eighty-Four by George Orwell. At all good bookshops.

The glossary

Jargon-free explanation

The glossary

Automatic Teller Machines (ATM) Bank cash point or hole-in-the-wall cash machine.

Biometric data This is data derived from distinctive bodily features such as fingerprints, photographs, iris patterns, signatures, palm vein recognition, gait and vocal characteristics and so on. Converting this data to digital form allows it to be processed automatically by computers.

Computerised Face Recognition (CFR) Systems that have the capacity to automatically compare faces captured on CCTV, using a database of facial images.

Community Legal Services Fund (CLS) Previously known as Legal Aid.

Driver and Vehicle Licensing Authority (DVLA) Based in Swansea, its database holds the name, address and other details of every driver in the country.

Dataveillance The matching of information gathered from surveillance with stored data e.g. matching facial images from a football crowd with a data bank of football hooligans.

Echelon A global intercept system which captures and analyses virtually every phone call, fax, email and telex message sent anywhere in the world.

Government Communications Head Quarters (GCHQ) The British government's listening station, the responsibility of the Joint Intelligence Committee. It is one of the world's most sophisticated intelligence gatherers.

Internet Service Providers (ISPs) Companies providing access to the Internet. This could be via the phone line, cable or satellite.

Joint Intelligence Committee (JIC) Part of the Cabinet Office, membership is made up of senior officials from the security, defence and foreign affairs agencies, responsible for providing government with co-ordinated interdepartmental intelligence assessments on a range of issues in the national interest.

Liberty An independent human rights organisation that works to defend and extend rights and freedoms in England and Wales.

Menwith Hill Near Harrogate, North Yorkshire, is the world's largest monitoring communications station.

Military Intelligence, section 5 (MI5) The British counter intelligence and security agency.

MI6 See entry under SIS.

Moore's Law States that the number of transistors on a computer chip (its power) would double every 24 months. The prediction, found to be correct, was made in 1965 by computer chip maker Intel's co-founder, Gordon Moore.

National Security Agency (NSA) The United States agency responsible for collecting and analysing foreign communications and intelligence.

PACE (Police and Criminal Evidence Act) Gives the police the right to stop and search any person on the street on the grounds of suspicion.

Privacy Enhancing Technologies (PETS) Encryption – converting sensitive information into a code that others can't understand – is its most obvious form.

Personal Identification Verification (PIV) Verification systems such as biometrics.

Radio Frequency Identification (RFID) Used primarily in retailing, these minute chips can be embedded into virtually anything from items of clothing to the human body and allow the object to be tracked. Tesco have already trialled them.

Secret Intelligence Service (SIS) British intelligence service, otherwise known as MI6, which traditionally operates abroad.

Telephone Management System (TMS) Which tracks patterns of telephone use and the destination of calls enabling management to detect employee's misuse.

Al Qaeda: the current threat
September 2008

Al Qaeda
the current threat

Frequent claims of foiled plots; tighter monitoring of suspects and stronger global terror laws. On the flip side, a new safe haven emerging for terrorists in Pakistan; stories of terror cells springing up throughout North Africa; numerous recruits from Europe's leading universities willing to sign up to the cause.

Are Al Qaeda and its affiliates, responsible for the horrific attacks in New York, London and Madrid, finding it hard to be the force they once were, or should we be bracing ourselves for the next outrage? Al Qaeda: the current threat weighs up the hard facts.

Author Paul Cruickshank, is a fellow at the Center on Law and Security at New York University and frequently provides analysis on Al Qaeda and international security concerns to CNN, the Guardian and the New Republic. He recently co-produced "Inside the Cell", an NBC investigation into the alleged plot to bring down airliners over the USA.

£6, 128 pages, October 2008, ISBN: 978-0-9554415-7-8

The Credit Crunch: how safe is your money?

July 2008

The Credit Crunch
how safe is your money?

Will the current credit crunch tip us into a global depression on a scale not seen since the 1920s? Are governments and central banks doing enough to alleviate uncertainty whilst juggling the threat of inflation? Is it time to hide our savings under the mattress?

The Credit Crunch: how safe is your money? checks the balance of the money markets and explains how a sub prime mortgage crisis in the USA has caused reverberations throughout global money markets, starting with the collapse of both Northern Rock in the UK and Bear Stearns in the US.

Author Simon Nixon heads up the Heard on the Street column for the Wall Street Journal. Prior to that he was executive editor of financial website Breaking Views, a founding editor of Money Week and is a regular contributor to The Spectator and The Independent.

£6, 112pages, July 2008, ISBN: 978-0-9554415-6-1

The Energy Crisis
April 2007

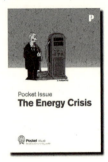

Oil is running out and costs are spiralling, fossil fuels pollute - so which way should the UK turn to fuel our future: is the UK right to be investing in nuclear power or should we rely on renewable energy sources?

The Energy Crisis tackles the big questions in a pithy pocket guide, helping you to sound knowledgeable when others don't.

Nathaniel Price is an author and writing consultant. He is also author of Pocket Issue, Global Warming and Pocket Issue, Middle East Conflict.

£4.99, 80 pages, April 2007, ISBN: 978-0-9554415-0-9

Food: what are we really eating?
December 2007

Is Organic food really better? Do we care more about Fairtrade or food miles? Are all e-numbers bad for us? Should we buy locally or from the supermarket?

Food: What are we really eating? lifts the lid on food production and gets you up-to-speed for your next weekly shop. Learn what's best for you, for the environment and to navigate through the myriad of choices: from organic, free-range, and fairtrade, to value and finest.

Mary Alexander is the author of Calling the Shots, a look at child-hood vaccination, of Pocket Issue, Pandemics and Pocket Issue, Fat. She is ghost author of the memoir, Call Me Elizabeth.

£4.99, 96 pages, December 2007, ISBN: 978-0-9554415-3-0

Also from Pocket Issue

Read up on other big global issues with these essential titles from Pocket Issue.

Al Qaeda: the current threat

The Credit Crunch: how safe is your money?

Drink & Drugs: culture of excess?

The Energy Crisis

Fat: eating ourselves to death?

Food: what are we really eating?

Global Warming

Middle East Conflict

Pandemics: bird flu, MRSA – should we be worried?

'Precisely what's needed...' Hephzibah Anderson, The Daily Mail

'For everyone who longs to be well-informed but lacks the time (or the attention span).' Alex Clark, The Observer

Pocket Issue is now available in Audio. Named the Sunday Times Audio Book of the Week, download your free sample at www.talkingissues.com.

Pocket ISSUE
Small briefs for a big world